Fiverr Secrets Unleashed

Copyright: Published in the United States by Kris McGee / © Kris McGee

Published 2014

All rights reserved. No part of this publication may be reproduced, stored in retrieval system, copied in any form or by any means, electronic, mechanical, photocopying, recording or otherwise transmitted without written permission from the publisher. Please do not participate in or encourage piracy of this material in any way. You must not circulate this book in any format. Kris McGee does not control or direct users' actions and is not responsible for the information or content shared, harm and/or actions of the book readers.

In accordance with the U.S. Copyright Act of 1976, the scanning, uploading and electronic sharing of any part of this book without the permission of the publisher constitute unlawful piracy and theft of the author's intellectual property. If you would like to use material from the book (other than just simply for reviewing the book), prior permission must be obtained by contacting the author at kmcgee@myownpixel.com – http://unlimitedincomesonline.com

Thank you for your support of the author's rights.

Fiverr Secrets Unleashed

Table of Contents

Fiverr Basics

Common Myths about Fiverr

Selling on Fiverr

Selling Secrets on Fiverr

15 Minute Gigs

Putting It All Together

Conclusion

Conclusion

Next Steps

Fiverr Basics

Beginning Fiverr

Fiverr is one of the biggest micro-job sites online today with thousands of buyers and sellers visiting the site daily. In fact, Alexa ranks the Fiverr.com website in the top 150 websites. Having this huge amount of traffic gives sellers a huge marketplace to sell. It only takes a few minutes to start your account and offering gigs to sell so what's stopping you?

The Fiverr platform basically is a marketplace for sellers to offer micro jobs or 'gigs' as they are referred to on Fiverr. From these gigs a buyer pays $5 for each one and the seller will receive $4 from that order. The 20% commission is also taken from higher priced gig extras as well. Once an order is complete it takes 14 days for the funds to clear on the Fiverr site then they can be withdrawn by Paypal or by using a prepaid debit card that Fiverr offers.

Creating an account and gigs are easy to do and lots of new people to Internet Marketing make their first money online using Fiverr. However, Fiverr can be a great way to make extra money and it's possible to also make a full time living on Fiverr.

Creating an Account

The first thing you'll need to do is create an account on Fiverr. However, there are a few things that you'll want to do when creating your account. Many guides I've read on Fiverr will advise to use keywords in your name, however, most of the top sellers don't employ this tactic and from the research I've done I don't think it helps much. Using a good friendly, easy to remember pen name is best.

The image you use on your account can say a lot about you as well. Try to use an image that promotes happiness. Images of a real person who is smiling or laughing works best on Fiverr. You can also use a company logo if you are using a branded company name. Some things to avoid are angry pictures, nudity, etc. Try to look professional in your profile pics.

For your bio, be sure to include keywords that you'll be targeting in your gigs. Also make sure you emphasize your previous experience and what makes you better than other sellers. Include any certificates or higher learning experience here.

Creating a Gig

Creating a gig is easy and can be done in just a few minutes. Here are some tips that can really help you create a better gig:

-Although there are 80 characters available in the title try to only use 60 or less and include a keyword related to the gig.

-Use related keyword throughout the description. Also take advantage of the highlight and text size styles to make key points of your gig stand out.

-Use specific keywords in your tags field. This can help promote your site better in early stages.

Changing the keywords and testing what works best can help you get the most gig views and orders

-Always use an image that attracts attention and looks professional. Take a look at some of the other related gigs to the one you're offering and try to match or beat them in terms of design and grabbing attention.

Common Myths about Fiverr

The Truth about Ebooks

Selling ebooks and downloadables on Fiverr can be successful in some cases. However, if you make and sell an ebook on Fiverr you'll also need to start investigating other sites to see if your ebook is offered there. Many times an ebook is copied and offered for a lesser price other sites. Although finding these sellers and contacting the sites to get the content removed is usually simple and easy to do it seems like a never ending battle.

If you plan on selling ebook it's best to make sure to put in ebook that the ebook is only available from Fiverr and that if a user bought the ebook from anywhere else but you to contact you and let you know. Many users will contact you and tell you where they got the ebook and you can take the necessary steps to get the content removed from these sites.

Make no mistake however that ebooks can be really profitable on Fiverr. It's best to research the best ebooks that are selling before you plan to write one however.

Using Multiple Accounts

Lots of sellers use multiple accounts on Fiverr. Although it's not specifically addressed in the terms of service as of this writing it's not a good idea. As a new seller you are given the ability to create and manage 20 gigs. With good research and constant testing and improving these 20 gigs can give you all the work you can handle. Once you gain top seller account status you'll be given more gigs space.

By only using a single account you focus on getting that account built up with reviews and promoting your top gigs. Many sellers with multiple accounts usually only have a few gigs that do well on these accounts and others are simply there.

You shouldn't need multiple accounts and should instead focus on a single account that you can promote your gigs and tweak to get more views and make more sales on your gigs.

Using Multiple Paypal Accounts

Although I don't promote using multiple accounts I decided to include this section for those who do want to use multiple accounts and get paid. Fiverr uses a Paypal account to pay once a gig is finished and the completion time has passed. In order to get paid each account must have its own paypal account. However, you can create up to 8 associated emails to your Paypal account. Simply use one of these 8 additional emails to receive the payment from Fiverr. This may be against the Terms of Service on Fiverr and could result in your account getting banned. I only included it here since so many people are using this method.

Trading Reviews and Buying Reviews

Many think that creating multiple accounts allows them to buy and review their own gigs however; Fiverr has cracked down on this. Reviews from the same IP are not counted and may not help you at all. In fact buying your own gig and rating it doesn't help your gigs and ends up costing you $1 for each review.

There are also many sites that offer trades for reviews. For example, you buy someone's gigs and give a review and they buy yours and then give you a review. Keep in mind however that Fiverr takes a 20% commission on sales so at very least these reviews cost $1 each.

There are ways to get reviews for new gigs which are covered in the Fiverr Secrets chapter of this ebook that can help you get reviews faster and without costing you anything.

Selling on Fiverr

Researching What Sells

One of the greatest things about Fiverr is the ability to see what's selling. You may not be able to get a really accurate number but it's easy to get a general idea of what to sell just by looking at what others are selling.

When you visit a profile on Fiverr there is a graph that shows how many orders the seller has received in the last month. The graph is called 'Recent Deliveries' and can give you an idea of how many gig orders a person gets each month. This does not include any gig extras that may have been ordered. So a seller who gets 100 orders a month should make at least $400 and maybe much more considering some gig extras can be as much as $100.

Once you find a seller who gets a good number of sales per month you can further your research to what they are selling. A great way to do this is by examining their feedback for each gig they offer. In my experience only half of the buyers leave feedback so if a gig receives 10 feedbacks per month it's likely the gig gets 20 orders per month.

Once you have a few ideas on what is selling on Fiverr that you can do it's time to create a gig that offers something similar, but better.

Recreating a Gig

Now that you've found a gig that you know sells on Fiverr and there are hungry buyers for it's time to create a gig. Examine other gigs that are selling and ranking high in the Fiverr search engine. Try to include many of the same keywords. You should not copy the description, title, or tags. Instead, try to make a more compelling call to action for your gig.

Make sure you include many related keywords in your description. You can also bold, highlight, and increase the size of the font on keywords to make them stand out. You are allowed 1200 characters in the description so be sure to use the entire space to promote your gig. Remember this is your chance to talk up your gig and make your buyer click the buy button.

If you're basing your gig on research you've done then offer a better deal than what's currently available. For instance, if a gig states it will give 100 links then you need to offer 150. Making your gig more appealing can catch the attention of buyers and that means more sales.

Building Reviews

Fiverr gigs are listed by how well received they are by buyers. You get reviews once your gig is delivered to the buyer. Better reviews mean better listing in the search results on on category pages. When you deliver your gig try to add something to your deliverable that will make the buyer want to give a review. A great way to do this is by including a bonus of some sort. Also ask the buyer if they aren't satisfied to let you know before leaving a review. It's better to refund an order in most cases than to take a negative review.

Building reviews is the best way to promote your gig in Fiverr search. There is also a sort by best rating on list pages such as categories so having a better rating means a higher result. In the next section I'll give you a few selling tips that can help you secure more sales and better ratings.

Selling Secrets on Fiverr

Secret 1 – Building reviews by Contacting Buyers

If you're basing your gig on another gig that you have researched then you know there are people who are interested and you know who they are. Simply look at the feedback and click on their username and you can contact a person that has bought a gig like yours recently.

If your gig is a better offer then send them a message with your gig details and tell them you would love to work with them on future projects. You can also offer a one-time bonus for trying your gig. Don't spam users mindlessly but craft messages that are personal and deal only with the gig they have purchased.

For new gigs this can really help to get some reviews going. It allows users to find your gig who are buyers.

Secret 2 – Sending Offers to Buyers

There is a page on Fiverr that has buyer requests. A great way to get reviews for your gigs is by sending offers to these buyers. You can promote your gig through your offer or as an additional service that they can benefit from.

The request section is located on the 'sales' page once you're logged into your account. If you're having a difficult time getting orders this page could help you get the ball rolling.

Secret 3 – Always Give a Bonus

No matter what you're selling it possible to give buyers a bonus. Make sure it's in the form of something other than what you're selling however. For instance, if you're selling Twitter followers send them a bonus which tells them how to get Facebook followers. Simply sending more than the advertised amount of something will not have as much impact although it's something that you should do as well. Consider the following example:

A buyer buys a 30 second testimonial video from 2 sellers and they both deliver the finished video on time.

Seller one delivers: a 38 second video and nothing else

Seller two delivers: a 34 second video and a text file that has instructions on how to quickly post the video to social sites. The text file also includes a gig that can promote the video in Youtube. Of course it's a gig that Seller 2 offers.

Chances are you're like everyone else and think that Seller 2 delivers more value even with the video being shorter. Simply because of the bonus text file that only takes a few seconds to add to the upload folder for delivery. It also adds an upsell for another gig that the seller offers which could results in more sales.

Secret 4 – Building a List on the Bonuses

Sending bonus files with your gigs can open many doors. You can offer something on your website like a free report after a user subscribes. For instance, if you sell SEO services on Fiverr like backlinks and send a bonus file that includes a link to your site that offers a free report then why not include it. Do not send your email or contact information in the bonus file however since this is against the Fiverr Terms of Service. However, you're not encouraging the user to contact you, instead you're attempting to give them something for free as a bonus for ordering your gig.

This is a great way to build your email list where you can promote other products as well. And the best part is you're making money just by building your list. You can also include a free report in your deliverable with links to affiliate products as well.

Secret 5 – Remove Negative Feedbacks

Getting a negative feedback on your gigs can really make it go down in rankings and hurt sales. If you receive a negative feedback there are a few things that you should do to try and get it removed. There are some buyers that will buy your gig and leave a negative feedback no matter what type of quality you deliver. They could be a competitor or just someone who can't be satisfied. Either way, if you're stuck with a negative feedback it's best to contact the buyer and ask them if you can help them so that they remove the feedback. If you don't get a response or they simply won't remove it offer them a refund. Even after you have delivered a job you can request a mutual cancel. If the order is cancelled then the feedback is removed.

If the buyer still refuses to remove the feedback and you've contacted them then you can contact the Fiverr support and ask for their help. This is hit and miss at best and it seems to depend on the mood of the reviewer but you can get feedback removed simply by stating your situation to the support staff. Let them know all the steps you've taken to try to satisfy the buyer including offering them a refund and they will likely remove the feedback for you.

Although its great to get feedback removed it's best not to depend on this and deliver your gigs on time and with everything you promised and more to avoid any negative feedbacks.

Secret 6 – Learn the Arbitrage Gigs

Many gigs on Fiverr can be bought cheaper from other places. If you want to successfully sell on Fiverr but you only want to be the 'middleman' then arbitrage may be for you.

You can buy gigs from places like SEOClerks.com or from other clone sites like Fiverr. Social signals are some of the best arbitrage products to sell on Fiverr.

Secret 7 – Always Use a Video

If your gig doesn't have a video explaining what it's about then you really need one. Gigs with videos are listed higher and get more orders. Fiverr clearly states this numerous times on their site. You can get a video made for free at animoto.com

Secret 8 – Withdraw More Than $50 to Save on Fees

Although this is not that much of a secret most sellers don't realize but when you withdraw more than $50 you're only charged $1 for Paypal fees. So you can save money by letting your profits accumulate and only withdrawing when it's more than $50.

15 Minute Gigs

How long should it take to complete a Gig?

Most users who are in countries like the USA, UK, or Australia will likely need to complete a gig in 15 minutes or less in order to make a decent income. However, for users in India or the Philippines where the cost of living is much lower they could spend more time on the gigs. Depending on your location you'll need to determine how much time you spend on a gig. Personally I try to finish a gig in less than 10 minutes from start to finish.

There are many gigs you can offer that doesn't require much time to complete including video testimonials and short promo videos. You can also offer services like writing or editing copy.

When you are determining how long it will take to deliver a gig be sure to include time it takes to upload to fiverr and process the entire order from start to finish. Sometimes just delivering large videos on fiverr and typing messages to buyers can take 5 minutes alone.

Putting It All Together

Now that we've been through the entire course it's time to put together all that you've learned and start your Fiverr journey. I'll outline each step below to guide you and give a few pointers along the way.

Creating an Account

Creating the account is easy and only takes a few minutes. Remember to enter your correct email including paypal email address which will be used in withdrawals. Include a picture of someone in a happy mood or a company logo. Avoid images that promote negativity or risqué in nature.

Researching a Gig

Look through the Fiverr site to find gigs that you can do. View the sellers profile to find out how many they are selling then review the individual gigs to determine the market for such a gig. There is no need to create a gig that doesn't sell. By doing proper research we can find out what sells best and try to recreate those gigs only offering better quality or quantity for the gig. Be sure to include keywords that are related to your gig in your profile as well.

Posting a Gig for Sale

Now that we have a profile created and a few target gigs to create it's time to create the listings for those gigs. We'll need an image that promotes a call to action and looks professional. You'll also need a short video explaining your gig. Gigs with videos get more hits and sales so including a video is a must.

For the description be sure to include your main keywords and related keywords. Utilize the entire limit of 1200 characters or at least close to it including and promoting your gig. Remember the buyer is right there all you need to do is convince them to order now.

For the tags be sure to include related keywords to your gig.

Adding Gig Extras

Although for new sellers the gig extras may not be an option but once you get to level one which takes ten sales with good feedback you can offer gig extras. Make sure your gigs have gig extras as they can really be a way to boost your earnings. Level 2 and Top Rated sellers can have gig extras that can be up to $100 on a single gig. Adding these gig extras only takes a minute and can make much more money than a just a single gig. One of the best gig extras is the 'extra fast' option. It gives you the ability to make money simply by delivering the gig early.

Getting Traffic to Gigs

Now that you've got the gig posted and ready to orders it's time to get some traffic to them. The following methods work really well for getting traffic to gigs and can help boost your gig to get reviews.

Post on Forums about Your Gigs

There are loads of forums that contain the question: "What's the best Fiverr gig for…". Searching for these forums and offering your gig is a great idea. You can even post links to your Fiverr gigs in forum signatures and more. Don't spam these forums with blatant advertising your Fiverr gigs however. Be smart and provide value to the conversation.

Post Your Gigs to Twitter and Facebook

Posting your gig to Twitter and Facebook are easy to do and can give you a huge boost in sales. Including @fiverr in your tweet can help bring attention to people who follow fiverr on Twitter as well.

Connect with Buyers from Feedbacks

As mentioned before you can connect with buyer who have purchased similar gigs offering your service. Be sure not to spam users using this method. However, it does allow you to reach laser targeted buyer who have purchased a gig you're offering recently.

Set up Google Alerts of Your Keywords

Setting up Google alerts to let you know when your keywords are used in an article or post you can comment on can give you lots of traffic as well. Simply go to alerts.google.com and set it up. This works great for catching those forum topics when they just begin.

Constantly Update Your Gigs

Fiverr gives you the ability to analyze traffic to your gigs through the sales panel. If a gig doesn't get much traffic then change things like title, keywords, and description in order to help give it a boost. If your gig gets loads of traffic but no one buys then consider changing the description and adding text that calls the user to action at the end.

Continuing to analyze and update your gigs will ensure they stay current and relevant in searches. Fiverr will sometimes give more weight to gigs that were recently updated or new in search results too so updates should be done on a constant basis.

Check the Request Section

Now that the gig is live and we're waiting on sales you can check the requests section of Fiverr. This can help get orders on those slow days when not as many sales are coming through. You can also boost traffic to your gigs simply by promoting the gigs to buyers through the request section.

Conclusion

I hope you have a much deeper knowledge of Fiverr and how to make money on Fiverr after reading my book. If you have any questions or comments be sure to connect with me on Twitter (@krismcge). Now that you have all the information of how to make money on Fiverr it's time to put that knowledge to use and start making money. You can start on Fiverr in just a few minutes and building successful gigs was outlined above so let's get started.

Thank you again for downloading this book!

I hope you enjoyed reading Fiverr Secrets Unleashed.

Finally, if you enjoyed this book, please take the time to share your thoughts and **post a review on Amazon**. It'd be greatly appreciated!

Thank you!

Next Steps

- Write me an honest review about the book – I truly value your opinion and thoughts and I will incorporate them into my next book, which is already underway.

Thank You!

www.ingramcontent.com/pod-product-compliance
Lightning Source LLC
Chambersburg PA
CBHW071731170526
45165CB00005B/2248